Turning pain into power and wounds into wisdom

I'm Not My Story

A Poetic Journey of Healing

SWAMINI B

www.ResiliencePoetry.com

I'm Not My Story: A Poetic Journey of Healing
Copyright © 2026 by Swamini B.
All rights reserved.

No part of this book may be reproduced, stored in a retrieval system, or shared in any form—electronic, mechanical, photocopying, recording, or otherwise—without prior written permission from the publisher, except for brief quotations in reviews or academic references.

Published by Resilience Poetry
www.resiliencepoetry.com

ISBNs:
Paperback: 979-8-9926355-0-8
eBook: 979-8-9926355-2-2
Hardcover: 979-8-9926355-1-5
Audiobook: 979-8-9926355-3-9

Library of Congress Control Number: 2025905017

Cover Design & Interior Illustrations by Mariam Shindauletova
Interior Formatting by Ian Koviak
Edited by Cherie Kephart and Meghan Fandrich

Disclaimer: This book is a work of poetry and personal expression. While inspired by real experiences, it is not intended as a substitute for professional advice, therapy, or medical care.

Printed in the United States of America

For permissions, inquiries, or bulk orders, please contact:
info@resiliencepoetry.com

Content Warning

This collection of poems reflects my journey of healing and thriving after enduring childhood sexual abuse. As you read, please be mindful that some poems may evoke strong emotions. I encourage you to approach this collection with care. Your well-being is important—take breaks if needed, and feel free to skip any content that feels overwhelming.

If you experience distress while reading, I encourage you to reach out to a trusted person or mental health professional. For additional support, please refer to the Resources section at the end of the book.

To Swami Dayananda Saraswati:

A Song of Gratitude

I came to study Vedanta
wanting to be free
and when my heart was breaking
you stood by me.

I had never met anyone
so honest, so kind
your compassion and care
restored my mind.

Even when I was at my worst
you were calm and clear
your patience and wisdom
lessened my fears.

No matter the distance
you took my calls
offering your support
every time I'd fall.

I was plagued by doubt
drowning in despair
and you revealed my worth
with such tender care.

Content Warning

This collection of poems reflects my journey of healing and thriving after enduring childhood sexual abuse. As you read, please be mindful that some poems may evoke strong emotions. I encourage you to approach this collection with care. Your well-being is important—take breaks if needed, and feel free to skip any content that feels overwhelming.

If you experience distress while reading, I encourage you to reach out to a trusted person or mental health professional. For additional support, please refer to the Resources section at the end of the book.

To *Swami Dayananda Saraswati:*

A Song of Gratitude

I came to study Vedanta
wanting to be free
and when my heart was breaking
you stood by me.

I had never met anyone
so honest, so kind
your compassion and care
restored my mind.

Even when I was at my worst
you were calm and clear
your patience and wisdom
lessened my fears.

No matter the distance
you took my calls
offering your support
every time I'd fall.

I was plagued by doubt
drowning in despair
and you revealed my worth
with such tender care.

You broke down my walls
taught me to listen
helped me to grow
to trust my intuition.

Oh, how I wish
you were still here to see
the freedom and joy
that now lives in me.

Thank you, Swamiji
for the gift you gave
your wisdom and guidance
made me brave.

You believed in me
when I couldn't find my way…
because of you
I cherish who I am today.

Introduction

I never thought I would find the courage to share my story. For years, I suffered in silence, convinced my secrets would be buried with me. But one day, while watching *American Idol*, a contestant's simple yet profound words struck a chord deep within me: "Everyone has a story; you just have to be a survivor of your story." In that moment, I realized I had not only survived but was thriving despite everything I'd been through.

That day marked a transformative moment in my life. I told my childhood friend the secret I had kept hidden from almost everyone: I'm a survivor of sexual abuse and was sold as a child.

Speaking my truth freed me in ways I never could have imagined. A wall within me began to crumble, and as I expressed the emotions that seeped through the cracks, the heaviness I had carried for so long transformed into a serene lightness.

My life has been a journey marked by both pain and privilege. While the pain of my past runs deep, I feel privi-leged because my longtime companions—shame, despair, and self-doubt—no longer weigh me down. Gone are the days when fear, mistrust, and judgment—both from others and myself—dominated my life. At sixty-six, I'm finally at peace and more content than I ever thought possible.

When I began doing the work to resolve my past, it felt like I was trapped in a dark tunnel, groping through darkness and losing my footing at every turn. I longed to find someone who had been through something similar and emerged on the other side. I needed reassurance that healing was attainable. Today, I'm honored to be the example I once needed.

This collection is my testimony to thriving after surviving. Through these poems, I offer an honest account of my journey towards self-acceptance. My goal is not to act as a guide but to extend a hand to fellow survivors who, like I once did, live with shame and fear of judgment.

My message is simple: healing is possible. We are not defined by our past. What happened to us does not have to dictate who we are today. Facing trauma is both challenging and courageous, but it can lead to inner freedom and peace. I'm living proof that such liberation is possible, and I sincerely wish the same for every survivor. I hope my poems inspire you to embark on your own healing journey and discover the strength and resilience that is an inherent part of you.

Contents

Content Warning
To Swami Dayananda Saraswati: A Song of Gratitude
Introduction

TURMOIL

Despair's Cry	12
Into the Void	13
Storm Within	14
Bound in Silence	15
Mother No Mother	16
Silent Agony Revealed	18
Dreams of Revenge	19
Facing the Cost	20
It's Up to Me	21
Braced for the Fight	22
Casting Off Shadows	23
Spring Cleaning	25
A Heart Reclaimed	26
Finding My Voice	27
Remembering Mattie	28
Light in the Abyss	30

INSIGHTS

Soaking in Solace	34
Floating Thoughts	36
The Need to Please	37
Past in Motion	38
Aligning Within	40
Relinquishing Self-Hate	42
I'm Not to Blame	43
Sensory Overload	44
Rising from Ruin	46
Checking Back In	47
Whispers of Wisdom	48
The Power of Choice	49
Mindful Mastery	51
Beyond Perfection	52
Behind the Veil	54
Forged by Fire	55
Shades of Truth	57
Chronic Clarity	59
Head No Longer Bowed	61

FREEDOM

My True Essence	65
Grateful for My Past	66
Nothing Left to Hide	67
Self-Redemption	69

Rising Strong	70
A Race Worth Running	71
Crafting My Path	72
Breathe and Reset	73
Cherished Moments	74
Sowing New Dreams	75
The Ceaseless Dance	76
Awakening to Wholeness	77
Unbroken Spirit	78
I Am Free	80
Heartfelt Thanks	81
Unburdened Heart	82
I Am More Than My Story	84
R.I.P.	86
Dear Reader	88
Survivors' Anthem	89
An Invitation	91

RESOURCES

24-Hour Hotlines	*93*
Organizations Advocating for Survivors	*96*
Online Resources	*99*
Reflections from Others	*101*

TURMOIL

G

Despair's Cry

A deep sorrow
grips my soul
a relentless ache
takes its toll.

My mind teeters
on the brink
like a ship in a storm
about to sink.

Into the silence
I scream in vain…
tears falling
like torrential rain.

Pain pierces
through to my core
I'm completely broken
sprawled out on the floor.

I must find a way
to lift this weight
before despair
dictates my fate.

Into the Void

Sinking into darkness
silence all around
lost in its vastness
only emptiness abounds.

No hope...
the hollowness chills my soul
I'm beyond the point
of being consoled.

No tunnel, no light
just black, binding pain
a deep-seated grief
etched in my brain.

No end in sight
no more fight...
just a fading ember
swallowed by night.

Storm Within

The rage I couldn't show
lay dormant
smoldering below.

Bursting forth
loathing
a fiery force.

Without warning
thoughts
began swarming.

An avalanche of emotion
my mind
a turbulent ocean.

Storm passed
heart
downcast.

Deeply dismayed
by choices
I made.

Bound in Silence

I was a victim
of countless crimes
yet no one was prosecuted
not one served time.

Subjected to
others' insanity
revenge became
a mental fantasy.

My desire for vengeance
a hidden flame
burning brightly
in a solitary game.

The rage I felt
they didn't know
behind silent eyes
I let it grow.

Mother No Mother

Why was there no room
for me in your heart?

Nobody knew
you hid your hatred well
allowing their cruelty
you made my life hell.

Deaf to my pleas
blind to my cries
you fed on my pain
with no compromise.

You watched as my soul
withered away
silent, complicit
demanding I obey.

So, I never had a mum
a mother only in name
at last, I see the truth:
not me… you are to blame.

But why was it so easy
to treat me with such disdain?
How could you be so cold
untouched by my pain?

Silent Agony Revealed

I hate my abusers
for what they did to me
and for making me take part
in their acts of cruelty.

Being forced to participate
in their heinous crimes
left me battered and broken
in both body and mind.

But now this reality
I'm ready to face
a new perspective
I choose to embrace.

I'm a survivor
of childhood sexual abuse.
Their crimes don't define me…
they're a part of my truth.

Dreams of Revenge

The pain they caused me
made my mind soar
in vivid dreams
I settled the score.

The fear on their faces
the whites of their eyes
I stood unmoved
numb to their cries.

Their pleading voices
echoed through the night
as I turned the tables
on my plight.

And when it was over
I walked away
knowing in dreams
I could make them pay.

Only when dreaming
was I bold and strong
it was the only place
I could right the wrong.

Facing the Cost

Though tough to grasp
I must break free
from my past.

As I face the staggering cost
it's heartbreaking to see
all I've lost.

I've aged and moved on
but trauma's grip
remains strong.

Old fears cloud my sight
paranoia and mistrust
fuel my fight.

Tired of succumbing to my past
I know it's my thinking
that I must recast.

It's Up to Me

I longed for someone
to take away the pain
desperate for relief
my search was in vain.

But now I know
I'll never find
someone to save me
from my mind.

Though many offered
comfort and hope
I'm the one
that must learn to cope.

I alone must face
the harsh reality
and deal with the effects
of my abusers' brutality.

And it's only when
I start to feel
that I'll unlock the door
and begin to heal.

Braced for the Fight

Stepping outside
I reaffirmed my vow
determined to stay safe
some way, somehow.

With every stride
my resolve grew strong
as I prepared to face
what lay beyond.

The scars of abuse
sharp and clear
phantoms alive
fed by fear.

This time
I'll stand my ground…
no matter what
I won't back down.

Casting Off Shadows

If I met someone
with my history
they'd have my respect…
then why not me?

They said I was worthless
breathing air I didn't deserve
destined for prison
a cell long reserved.

Their venomous words
took their toll
casting shadows
across my soul.

Consumed
by their projections
I drowned in the weight
of their imperfections.

Their lies entwined
distorting my mind
yet a spark of hope
I sought to find.

Writing revealed a truth
I couldn't deny
in facing my pain
I saw through the lie.

Spring Cleaning

I'm cleaning out my closet
on a mission to explore
the parts of myself
hidden behind closed doors.

Not pretending to be normal
whatever that may mean
making choices
that elevate my self-esteem.

I'm no longer ashamed
go on, judge me if you please
I'm done hiding
I'm recovering from this disease.

Throwing out self-doubt
scrubbing away fear
making room
for a life that's sincere.

A Heart Reclaimed

Most of my choices
were fueled by self-hate
but today, I'm letting go
of that oppressive weight.

By breaking my silence
and placing blame where it's due
I've discovered traits
that I never knew.

I'm capable of love
and have a kind heart
generous in spirit
I now honor every part.

I can also be stubborn
opinionated and dismissive
but to self-hate
I'm no longer submissive.

Finding My Voice

From the world
I tried to hide
the thoughts and feelings
that I denied.

Fearful of people
invading my space
never truly
feeling safe.

Yet through these poems
I'm finding relief
from years of anguish
and deep-seated grief.

By voicing
what I think and feel
I release the pain
and let my heart heal.

Through the power of poetry
I've set my spirit free
unafraid and unashamed
to face my reality.

Remembering Mattie

Recalling past trauma
can be brutal…
for some of my friends
it was fatal.

A harsh
and unyielding truth
that robbed Mattie
of her youth.

Her flashbacks were fierce
yet her kindness shone through
she spoke with warmth
despite the battles she knew.

I admired her spirit
but I was blind
to the silent agony
that plagued her mind.

When she lay down
on that train track
it took me a while
to find my way back.

Mattie's death
shook me to the core...
a haunting reminder
of inner battles ignored.

Light in the Abyss

Unable to bear
life's crushing weight
I was devastated
by the hands of fate.

No respite from mind's
relentless debating
drowning in sorrow
slowly suffocating.

The searing sorrow
was more than I could take
so I sought an end
a final escape.

But in that vast abyss
a light broke through…
a voice softly whispered
"I'm here with you."

Finding myself alive
that Monday night
I regained my strength
and power to fight.

I made a promise
to myself that day:
never again will I attempt
to throw my life away.

INSIGHTS

Soaking in Solace

At times I'd take
up to eight baths a day
only when submerged
did I feel safe, not prey.

The bathroom, my refuge
shielded my back
protecting me from
sudden attacks.

Violated regularly
I always felt dirty
yet deep inside
I yearned for purity.

The water scalding
my attempt to cleanse
the stains of abuse
I sought to transcend.

Unable to escape
often frozen in fear
hot baths were a way
I eased my despair.

But now when I bathe
I feel serene...
no more purging in hot water
Today, I know that I'm clean.

Floating Thoughts

Like clouds drifting high above
thoughts in my mind
push and shove.

Always in ample supply
they roam about freely
and multiply.

As I learn to face both light and storm
the shape of my past
will transform.

Then one day, just like a tranquil sky
thoughts will arise, linger a while
then silently float by.

The Need to Please

Caught in a cycle
of needing to please
my own desires
left unappeased.

Supporting others
I justified my worth
seeking validation
through selfless work.

I suffered from
low self-esteem
it was only when giving
that I felt redeemed.

But the ache inside
burned like a flame
a deep longing
I couldn't name.

Past in Motion

When past and present
overlapped
I'd find myself
in a familiar trap.

Lost in a world
I once knew
old memories
distorting my view.

Unresolved emotions
I had to allow
confusing... for no one
is hurting me now.

Realizing some emotions
don't belong in the present
I'm figuring out
which ones are relevant.

By grounding myself
in who I am today
I'm watching old fears
slowly fade away.

Emotions rise
and then depart
no longer holding dominion
over my heart.

With conscious effort
I take the reins
refusing to yield
to past-born pain.

Now when emotions
suddenly appear
I confront them boldly
with courage, not fear.

Aligning Within

Tired of being bound
to a past that's dead
I'm breaking free
from the cage in my head.

Absolute consistency
was once my decree
now I see the cost
of my rigidity.

I'm trying to accept others
as they are
not through the filter
of old inner scars.

Fewer reactions
more thoughtful replies
no longer seeking perfection
in flawless ties.

I'm harmonizing
both the inner and outer
letting my inner wisdom
grow louder.

Aligning my heart
with the values I hold
I breathe... reflect...
let awareness unfold.

Relinquishing Self-Hate

The scars on my skin
reveal the depths
of the torment
once buried within.

Forced to inflict pain
I couldn't cope
though under their control
I never lost hope.

I rejected their ways
and all they stood for
vowing to be different
driven by something more.

My whole life
I've worked to free my mind
conquering the images
that kept me confined.

Now, from self-hate
I've broken free
their actions are theirs...
they don't define me.

I'm Not to Blame

I'm not responsible
for the choices they made
nor for the price I paid.

I'm not responsible
for what they did to me
nor for what they forced me to be.

Today, I'm standing tall
reclaiming my voice
my power, my all.

I will not accept their guilt
nor will I accept their shame
and I won't remain silent.

I'm not to blame.

Sensory Overload

Why did I overreact
to cold, smell, and taste
or lose it when a sound
entered my space?

Why were my reactions
so extreme
negatively impacting
my self-esteem?

Instantly I'd lose
my composure
without understanding
what took over.

And I knew it affected
everyone around
when space in my mind
could not be found.

After researching
I now know
the sensory part of my brain
didn't develop and grow.

This mode of adapting
is not unique to me
it's common among trauma
survivors... just like me.

Rising from Ruin

Raised by my family
to be a reject in society
I yearned to break free
from their impropriety.

Fleeing from a past
I condemned
I stumbled, trying
to be different from them.

Embracing my story
without resistance
I've let go of the need
to justify my existence.

Determined to create a life
I truly desire
I'm shedding habits
that diminish my inner fire.

No longer shackled
by my family's fears
shattering these bonds
I will persevere.

Checking Back In

I had no idea
I'd checked out of life
silently suffering
hope lost to strife.

My perception of the world was
difficult to shift
futile thoughts
I couldn't resist.

Once pessimistic
at times fatalistic
now self-aware
I'm proudly optimistic.

Here I am at sixty-six
with strength I can't ignore
with courage as my companion
the world I'll bravely explore.

Free to pursue my dreams
the path before me open
ready to forge ahead
no longer broken.

Whispers of Wisdom

It still astonishes me to see
how my past molded me.

I thought by confronting
old feelings and fears
I would be safe from
further chaos and tears.

But it wasn't only my childhood
I needed to resolve
my current behavior
had to evolve.

Anchoring my attention
in the present moment
turned out to be
extremely potent.

Now that I'm aligning
with my true nature
my inner voice
I can hear and nurture.

The Power of Choice

The quality of my life
is something I choose
my thoughts determine
if I heal or stay bruised.

Questioning patterns
that no longer ring true
I release the ones
that influenced my view.

Thinking before speaking
tempers my reactions
creating space
for meaningful interactions.

Deciding with care
which thoughts I'll entertain
is much easier now
my mind has been trained.

As thoughts ebb and flow
like waves riding the tide
I engage with life
with awareness as my guide.

Firm in resolve
I chart my course
like a ship sailing
with a calm steady force.

Mindful Mastery

I am not my thoughts
I am not my mind.

I observe my thoughts
I use my mind.

Beyond Perfection

I'm fighting for
the ultimate prize
where valor resides
and liberty thrives.

The freedom to reveal
the depths of my soul
authentic living
has become my goal.

Behind the facade
of perfection's allure
knocking down my walls
I feel safe and secure.

Honoring my virtues
and owning my flaws
has freed me from
self-made laws.

In this dance of life
I choose to be bold
trusting the journey
letting my story unfold.

With each new dawn
I welcome what's in store
honoring a truth
my soul can't ignore.

Behind the Veil

Life's challenges are neutral
it's my projections
that made them feel futile.

Futile yet feeling real
behind a veil of fear
my truth was concealed.

Concealing truths I needed to resolve
the pain of silence
forced me to evolve.

Evolving led to the discovery
inner strength
now fuels my recovery.

Recovering from shame and judgement
I stand in my power
no longer hesitant.

Forged by Fire

Once called a diamond
unpolished, unrefined
forged by fire
I've reclaimed what's mine.

I now see myself as
resilience reborn
shining brightly
having weathered the storm.

Seeing struggles
as moments of growth
I've learned to rise
and honor them both.

Facing life head-on
with steady resolve
I know these trials
have helped me evolve.

Once uncertain
now grounded and sure
my mind resolute
my spirit is secure.

What a privilege
to stand in this place
at peace with my past
rooted in grace.

Shades of Truth

Religion once served
as my escape
helping me
reshape my fate.

With its code
of conduct to live by
I made decisions
I could justify.

But idealism soon became
my addiction
masking my tendency
toward self-restriction.

Unaware of my need
to confine and control
I focused solely
on saving my soul.

I was convinced I knew
wrong from right
until life showed me
it isn't just black and white.

Boundaries, a mystery
I didn't comprehend
yet my beliefs
I'd fiercely defend.

To liberate myself
from these afflictions
I had to confront
my trauma-driven convictions.

Realizing my views
were problematic
I sought a perspective
more pragmatic.

No longer seeking refuge
or needing to escape
I stand in my truth
fully awake.

A spiritual person
a seeker of truth
sculpted by the trials
that shaped my youth.

Chronic Clarity

With newfound insight
I understand the toll
the autoimmune battle
that once took control.

Rheumatoid arthritis
was the price I paid
silent agony
externally displayed.

This disease, a sign
my body's quiet plea
a symptom of turmoil
deeply rooted in me.

Endless days trapped
in fight or flight
from morning's first glow
to the stillness of night.

Looking back
it's clear to see
why my body
rebelled against me.

Recognizing the link
between thoughts and pain
I'm actively rewiring
pathways in my brain.

When old habits
creep into the day
I can spot the patterns
that once led me astray.

Now my body can rest
and begin to repair…
the pain loses power
when I'm fully aware.

Head No Longer Bowed

For many years
I hid behind a disguise
veiled in shadows
blinded by lies.

Mustering the courage
to face my fears
unleashed a torrent
of unshed tears.

Tears released and
my story told
at last, I'm free
from my mind's stronghold.

Liberated from
my painful past
I stand in my truth
with hope unsurpassed.

Triumphant through
each test and trial
I now know
it was all worthwhile.

Today I stand before you
victorious and proud
head held high
no longer bowed.

FREEDOM

My True Essence

In this journey
of self-discovery
I've awakened
a hidden part of me.

It exists independent
of my mind
a gem so rare
I'm grateful to find.

Speaking with
a distinctive voice
it guides me through
every choice.

It's my authentic self
my inner guide
how I see myself
has been redefined.

A companion
on which I now depend
dearer to me
than my closest friend.

Grateful for My Past

Breaking my silence
and owning my story
resilience now radiates
in all its glory.

Though I wouldn't want
to relive the past
I'm proud of the strength
I have amassed.

Through darkness I walked
toward the dawn
with each step
an inner strength was born.

Honoring each facet
of my evolving self
I turned pain into power
and embraced my true wealth.

I'm truly amazed
that I can say
it's because of my past
I am who I am today.

Nothing Left to Hide

Now that there's nothing
left to hide
I feel a pride
that flows from inside.

In awe of my journey
despite my plight
I honor my spirit
my will to fight.

As I crossed each bridge
hope would rise
with each step forward
fear met its demise.

No longer struggling
just to survive
I'm grateful for the gift
of feeling truly alive.

Voicing my truth
the impossible became possible
my inner wisdom
is surprisingly audible.

Internally guided
hidden truth exposed
I walk unafraid
heart open, not closed.

Self-Redemption

I wish I'd known
it wasn't my fault
escapism wouldn't
have been my default.

My true self
I wouldn't have hidden
nor lived in fear
panic-stricken.

I ran so far
from my core
spinning in a spiral
that kept me unsure.

From the shattered pieces
I healed my heart
emerged from the rubble
to create this work of art.

With each word I write
I'm carving my path
telling a story
that's mine to craft.

Now I know, none of it was my fault
self-respect is my new default.

Rising Strong

No longer adrift
no longer out of control
I fought, I won...
my spirit is whole.

No more wandering
no more strife
I've found my way
to a balanced life.

I've battled hard
with hope by my side
now in this world
I'm my own guide.

My peace is a victory
that I have earned
in finding my voice
the tides have turned.

A Race Worth Running

I feel like the tortoise
who won the race
steadily moving
at my own pace.

Emerging from shadows
resolve my shield
armed with courage
my capacity revealed.

Running this race
was a blessing in disguise
perseverance has
opened my eyes.

Like the one who triumphed
I'm now assured
whatever comes next
I will endure.

Crafting My Path

Freed from the asteroids
my past left behind
I now observe
the orbits of my mind.

No longer pulled
to thoughts like gravity
I move with ease
inviting clarity.

Challenges arise
like meteors in flight
but with cosmic calm
I rise to new heights.

Trusting my inner stars
to light the way
even in stormy skies
I'll be okay.

This shift in awareness
has allowed me to see
I'm in control
of my destiny.

Breathe and Reset

Now that body, mind
and soul are aligned
my disease no longer
consumes my mind.

If nothing new happens
I know it's my fears
making the pain worse
inducing my tears.

The intensity reminds me
to pause and regroup
free my mind from
that habitual pain loop.

I say to my brain,
"Let's reset and refocus
entertaining these thoughts
will make you feel hopeless."

Renouncing the habit
of feeding the pain
I breathe deeply
until calm floods my veins.

Cherished Moments

With a grateful heart
I cherish each day
delighting in nature's
awesome display.

Listening to the ocean's
gentle call
watching the sunset
as shadows fall.

Through smiles, struggles
and moments sublime
I treasure this precious
life of mine.

Sowing New Dreams

I didn't expect life
to give me a fresh start
yet it surprised me
and healed my heart.

Choosing with care
which seeds to sow
as I pursue my dreams
self-confidence grows.

Reflecting on what
brings me peace
musts and *shoulds*
quietly cease.

Free to choose
what nurtures my soul
I am living fully
feeling whole.

In this garden of life
I'm starting to play
with love and laughter
guiding my way.

The Ceaseless Dance

Once a chaotic river
my mind is now a tranquil sea…
immersed in its stillness
I enjoy clarity.

With inner wisdom
aligning my energy
thoughts and emotions
drift by effortlessly.

Awareness stirs sensations
that ebb and flow
fleeting impressions
that come and go.

In moments of stillness
as truth begins to rise
I'm gently guided
my mind unified.

In a ceaseless dance
where harmony resides
I've learned to flow
with life's shifting tides.

Awakening to Wholeness

What did I uncover by looking within?
I found a part of me that remained pure and whole.

A part allowing me to observe my mind.

A part I trust as my inner guide.

A part connected to the rest of life.

A part where I can rest inside.

A part that accepts life as it is.

A part open to what life brings.

A part that knows I am not my story.

A part grateful for this transformative journey.

Unbroken Spirit

In shadows deep
silence emanates
a heart-wrenching grief
hard to penetrate.

A childhood stolen
innocence betrayed
yet my spirit
refused to be caged.

Sold and abused
stripped of my rights
despite it all
I reached for new heights.

Refusing to be like them
or mirror their pain
I reclaimed my life
I broke every chain.

Finding a part of myself
untouched by the abuse
turning wounds into wisdom
I paid my dues.

Sharing my story
no longer constrained
I hope to inspire others
to rise above their pain.

I Am Free

My soul now soars
wild and free
bathed in the brilliance
of simply being me.

In self-love I've grown
to myself I commit
victoriously I celebrate
the light I emit.

My mind takes flight
my heart shines bright
resplendent I bask
in my being's pure light.

In this new chapter
I'm in control
a shining example
of a liberated soul.

Heartfelt Thanks

So many people
helped me along the way...
without your support
I wouldn't be here today.

To my spiritual family
caretakers, and friends
the doctors, therapists, and nurses
on whom I've come to depend.

Your impact on me
has been profound...
because you cared
my authentic self I've found.

I stand in awe
with a grateful heart
your love and compassion
played a vital part.

Your unwavering support
carried me through
and for that
I'll always be indebted to you.

Unburdened Heart

I hated my mum and dad
for a long, long time
but today I can separate
their lives from mine.

I'm amazed I can say this
with a quiet smile
my thoughts have softened
they're no longer hostile.

Moving past the hurt
I released the pain
opened my heart
and relinquished blame.

For far too long
I clung to resentment
recycling the pain
that fueled discontent.

My mind and body
bore the weight
until I chose to heal
and reshape my fate.

I've accepted the lot
I was given
and did the work
to start truly living.

Widening my vision
allowed me to see
their brokenness
never did define me.

I Am More Than My Story

I'm not the tears
that once flowed freely
nor the story
that blinded me.

I'm not the wounds
or the fight
nor the battles
fought in the night.

I'm not the lies
I once believed
nor the whispers
that had me deceived.

There's a spark
darkness didn't steal
an inner light
grief couldn't conceal.

I am the stillness
beyond the sound
the quiet space
where truth is found.

I am the witness
to the storm
the place within
where healing is born.

I'm like the ocean
vast and wide
I'm the eternal observer
unshaken inside.

I'm not my story
I am the soul…
reclaimed, reborn,
and in control.

December 31, 2024

my abuse story died

R.I.P.

January 1, 2025

like a phoenix,

I rise

Dear Reader,

I want to express my deepest gratitude for taking the time to engage with my journey through poetry. This collection is a living testament to survival and transformation.

Writing these poems has been a life-changing experience—one that allowed me to face my past, embrace my truth, and step into a life of clarity and peace. To know that you have read them, felt them, and perhaps even recognized parts of your own story within them means more than I can express.

Thank you for your openness, your time, and for allowing my words to resonate with you. I hope that within these pages, you have found inspiration, healing, and the courage to walk your own path with strength and grace.

With gratitude,
Swamini B.

Survivors' Anthem

Don't give up
don't ever back down
there's a strength inside you
waiting to be found.

Life can be hard
yet you've pushed through
because you didn't yield
this anthem is for you.

Each moment you endure
every breath you take
is a stand against the darkness
a choice that you make.

Though the fight is hard
stay true to your quest
with resilience as armor
you'll conquer the rest.

Remember this truth:
you're not alone
together we rise
our strength is our own.

So, lift your voice
let this anthem ring true
you're a survivor…
there is power in you.

Hold tight to this message
let it lift you each day
you're stronger than your past
in every way.

An Invitation

If you'd like to continue the journey, I've created two free offerings to support reflection and connection—both available on my website:

- A downloadable **gratitude journal**

- An **audio sample** of selected poems, read aloud in my voice

You can access both directly at www.ResiliencePoetry.com No sign-up required. Just come as you are.

With love and respects,
Swamini B.

Scan to access the Gratitude Journal
and Audio Sample

RESOURCES

For immediate emergencies,
please call 911

24-Hour Hotlines

Childhelp National Child Abuse Hotline
 1-800-4-A-CHILD (1 800-422-4453)
 childhelp.org
Provides crisis intervention, information, and referrals for child abuse cases.

Crisis Text Line
 Text "HELLO" to 741741
 crisistextline.org
Provides support via text message for people in crisis.

LGBT National Help Center
 1-888-843-4564
 lgbthotline.org
Provides telephone, online chat, and email peer support for LGBTQ individuals.

National Domestic Violence Hotline
 1-800-799-SAFE (7233)
thehotline.org
Offers support and resources for individuals experiencing domestic violence and those who have experienced sexual abuse.

National Human Trafficking Hotline
📞 1-888-373-7888
🌐 humantraffickinghotline.org
Support for victims of human trafficking and public information.

National Sexual Assault Hotline (RAINN)
📞 1-800-656-HOPE (4673)
🌐 rainn.org
Confidential support from trained staff (Rape, Abuse & Incest National Network).

National Suicide Prevention Hotline
📞 1-800-273-TALK (8255)
🌐 suicidepreventionlifeline.org
Support for people in distress and prevention resources.

Stop It Now
📞 1-888-PREVENT (773-8368)
🌐 stopitnow.org
Resources and support to prevent child abuse.

The Trevor Project
📞 1-866-488-7386
🌐 thetrevorproject.org
Crisis intervention and suicide prevention for LGBTQ youth.

988 Suicide & Crisis Lifeline
📞 Phone or Text: 988
🌐 988lifeline.org
Support for people in suicidal crisis or emotional distress.

Organizations Advocating for Survivors

Brave Movement
🌐 bravemovement.org
Global movement to end childhood sexual violence and support survivors.

Darkness to Light
🌐 d2l.org
Prevents child abuse by educating adults on protection strategies.

Enough Abuse Campaign
🌐 enoughabuse.org
Education and training to prevent child abuse and reduce risk factors.

Help for Adult Victims of Child Abuse (HAVOCA)
🌐 havoca.org
Support and advice for adults affected by child abuse.

The International Society for the Study of Trauma and Dissociation (ISSTD)
🌐 isst-d.org
Public education, clinical training, and trauma-related research.

The Lamplighter Movement
🌐 thelamplighters.org
Resources and support for survivors of sexual abuse and their families.

MaleSurvivor
🌐 malesurvivor.org
Support for male survivors through advocacy and resources.

National Alliance to End Sexual Violence
🌐 endsexualviolence.org
Advocates for policies to end sexual violence and support survivors.

The National Child Traumatic Stress Network (NCTSN)
🌐 nctsn.org
Raises care standards and access for traumatized children and families.

National Children's Alliance (NCA)
🌐 nationalchildrensalliance.org
Coordinates services for child victims of abuse through Children's Advocacy Centers.

Prevent Child Abuse America
🌐 preventchildabuse.org
Promotes services to improve child well-being and prevent abuse.

Stop the Silence
🌐 stopthesilence.org
Prevents child abuse through awareness, education, and policy.

Survivors Network of those Abused by Priests (SNAP)
🌐 snapnetwork.org
Support for survivors of clergy sexual abuse.

Online Resources

1in6
🌐 1in6.org
Support for men who have been abused, including online resources.

Adult Survivors of Child Abuse
🌐 ascasupport.org
Self-help programs for adult survivors of abuse.

After Silence
🌐 aftersilence.org
Online support group for survivors of rape and sexual abuse.

The Healing Journey
🌐 thehealingjourney.org
Recovery tools and communities for survivors of sexual abuse.

The Joyful Heart Foundation
🌐 joyfulheartfoundation.org
Support for abuse survivors through healing programs and advocacy.

The National Center for Victims of Crime
🌐 victimofcrime.org
Support, advocacy, and resources for victims of all crimes.

The National Sexual Violence Resource Center (NSVRC)
🌐 rainn.org
Training and resources to prevent and respond to sexual violence.

Pandora's Project
🌐 pandys.org
Support for survivors of sexual abuse, including online groups.

Survivors of Incest Anonymous (SIA)
🌐 siawso.org
12-step program for adult survivors of childhood sexual abuse.

Take Back the Night Foundation
🌐 takebackthenight.org
Ends sexual violence through awareness events and survivor support.

Voices In Action, Inc.
🌐 voicesinaction.org
Support and advocacy for survivors of childhood sexual abuse.

Reflections from Others

Each poem pulses with hard-won wisdom and emotional honesty, reminding us that we are not bound by our wounds or the stories we once believed about ourselves. We are all capable of shedding the weight of the past, reclaiming our voice, and stepping into freedom.

— Dr. Christina Donaldson,
Licensed Clinical Psychologist

From the ruins of unspeakable abuse rises a voice unflinching and luminous… *I'm Not My Story* pulses with raw truth, aching beauty, and grace. This book is not only a testimony—it's an anthem of survival, a lighthouse for anyone seeking peace in the shadow of trauma.

— Cherie Kephart, award-winning author of
A Few Minor Adjustments

Your manuscript made me cry. The changes you made, the subtle differences in word choice and line structure, the new images you integrated, are all beyond perfect. I think this was the best experience I've ever had as a poetry editor.

— Meghan Fandrich, editor

As a survivor, I felt deeply seen and supported in her words. The simplicity and clarity of her voice are deeply comforting, like a quiet companion who understands without needing to explain. It's rare to feel this held by a book.

— Diana Wallace, survivor

I'm Not My Story: A Poetic Journey of Healing is a masterclass in surviving and thriving. I saw myself in these pages. Swamini doesn't shy away from her trauma, but she doesn't stay there either. She shows the way through.

— Lorena Z., trauma survivor

I'm Not My Story allows the reader to cry, release, and breathe. It reminds us that our pain and trauma do not define us. Each poem is the voice of someone who knows what it is to hurt and what it means to heal. It offers grace, openness, and a gentle reminder that trust and healing are possible.

— Mary H., trauma survivor

This book has changed my life. The author's story is so inspir-ing, and it gives hope and faith that even after suffering so much, you can transform the pain into love and happiness. My utmost respect to all those who have experienced abuse and continue to move forward.

— Adriana Riccomini, survivor

Reading this book saved my life. I never knew someone could understand and put into words what I could never say. This book gave my experience a voice. Thank you for helping me heal.

— Zineb Bouhamidi, trauma survivor

As a survivor of abuse, not only as a child but also as an adult, I found profound strength and vulnerability in her words. No matter where you are in your healing journey, these poems guide you along a path of strength, growth, and liberation from inner demons.

For many of us, it can take a lifetime of self-sabotage before we find peace within. This collection reminds us that we are not alone, and that it is possible to overcome whatever life places in our path. Thank you for sharing your story and for helping others feel less alone.

— J. Hernandez, survivor